Unfolding a Boarder's Life

Tears, Trophies, and the Truth about Boarding Life

Nikhar Nema

Content

Foreword

When I first thought about writing this book, I wasn't sure if my story was special enough. But then I realised—every boarding student has a story, and this one is mine.

Boarding isn't just a school—it's a whole world with its own rules, people, and challenges. It's the place where I discovered how strong I could be, even when I missed home, failed, cried, or felt completely alone.

This book is not about perfection. It's about the real stuff—the failures, the small wins, the secret cashew missions, the 5:30 AM alarms, the moments of joy with friends, and the teachers who quietly shaped me.

If you've ever felt out of place, or had to adapt to something new, I hope this book makes you feel seen. Because it's not just a story about boarding. It's a story about growing up.

Preface

I didn't start writing this book with the intention of becoming an author. I started writing because I didn't want to forget.

There were so many moments—big and small—that shaped me in boarding school. Some made me laugh, some made me cry, and some taught me things no textbook ever could.

Soon, I realised that maybe my journey could also help others who are just starting out in boarding, or in any new phase of life. If you've ever been scared of change, struggled to fit in, or tried to find your voice in a loud world—this book is for you.

Writing this helped me understand myself better. I hope reading it does the same for you.

Acknowledgments

This book wouldn't exist without the people who believed in me, even when I didn't.

To my **parents**, thank you for trusting me with decisions that even I wasn't sure about. Every word in this book is a small way of saying—I'll keep trying to make you proud.

To **Shubhra Ma'am**, your strictness was a gift in disguise. You didn't just shape my routine; you shaped my character.

To **Vaishali Ma'am**, thank you for supporting me quietly but powerfully. You never gave up on me, and I'll always carry that with me.

To **Shweta Manyala Ma'am**, who encouraged me to write, helped me polish my story, and always pushed me a little further—you've been more than a teacher; you've been a mentor.

To my friends **Yash** and **Krishna**, who turned boarding from a hostel into a home—thank you for being my constants. And to every teacher, dorm-mate, and classmate who became a part of this journey—this book has bits of all of you.

Prologue

When I first walked into my boarding school, I didn't know that I was also stepping into the most life-changing chapter of my life. I thought it would be about studies, sports, and school uniforms. But it turned out to be about much more.

It was about losing things and learning how to find them again. About fighting sleep but waking up stronsger. About being afraid of the unknown and still choosing to show up.

There were tough days and even tougher nights. But in between, there were secret laughs, proud moments, new friendships, and tiny lessons that quietly stayed with me. This book is not a guide to surviving boarding life. It's just the story of how I did and maybe, just maybe—it'll help someone else do the same.

Chapter 1: The Decision

I think it was yesterday when I visited a large boarding school in Bhopal. My parents were very satisfied with the school, and they decided to put me there. Some of my family members were against the decision, but my parents had seen the changes in students before and after going to boarding. As boarding students don't get much time to spend with their family, we planned a trip to enjoy our best and last moments before I joined.

We went to a place known as *Paradise on Earth*—yes, you guessed it—Kashmir, in the lap of the Himalayas. The most beautiful moments of my life were spent there. It was a five-day trip. After that, only a week was left before I left for boarding. I was flooded with thoughts—curious and excited about the new life, new friends, but also nervous about surviving without my parents and doing chores I had never done, like washing my clothes or organizing my books.

Chapter 2: First Impressions

I still remember—it was 13th March when I entered the boarding. Everything looked dull, but I was still curious to explore. I walked into my room and saw a strict-looking lady. She completely ignored me as if I were invisible.

"Hello, aunty," a boy said as he entered the room while my mother was organizing my cupboard. He was my batchmate—Yash. Two or three more boys entered, looking strange to me at first, unaware that they would soon become my best friends.

As my parents finished setting up my cupboard, they spoke to that same lady, who turned out to be my warden. Then they left me to join the sports session. I felt happy—as if I had earned liberty. But something unexpected was about to happen.

That evening, I tasted the boarding school's dining food for the first time—it was good. One boy stood out—he was friendly and helpful. I thought he'd become one of my best friends, but he turned out to be the worst. That's the beauty of boarding life—no one shows their true colours at first.

Life in boarding is for the mentally strong. The book of life written in the ink of challenges had just begun to unfold…

Chapter 3: Shubhra Ma'am

In the boarding, I learned we had to wake up at 5:30 AM. That sounded like a Herculean task. But when I woke up and stepped out, I breathed fresh air and watched my first sunrise. It felt magical.

That strict lady? Her name was **Mrs. Shubhra**. I felt like she was biting me with discipline, but unknowingly, she was becoming the hero of my story.

Shubhra Ma'am was a pure-hearted and principled individual—something I came to realise in my second year. She had a strong dislike for undisciplined behaviour and held deep respect for students who were willing to listen and learn. Obedience and sincerity were qualities she admired, which is why she often found it difficult to connect with students who were overly stubborn. Her expectations were high, but they came from a place of genuine care and a desire to see us grow.

At the end of my second year in boarding, I realised Shubhra Ma'am had shaped me into a more disciplined and responsible person. She transformed me from a raw, stubborn rock into something polished—like a diamond. Strict yet purposeful, she believed in tough love.

Her discipline was never without reason. Through her actions, she taught me life lessons—how to treat others with respect and how to understand people's behaviour. She wasn't just a warden; she was a silent mentor.

Chapter 4: Struggles and Survival

I was very happy living in the boarding house independently without my parents. But suddenly, one of my most vital things—my notebook—was lost. I was neither in the habit of finding things nor had I ever lost them at home. You must be thinking, why is this notebook so vital? But it mattered a lot to me. When I had lost all hope of finding it, suddenly, tears started rolling out of my eyes. It was the moment when I remembered my parents the most. That night, I just calmed myself and had a sound sleep.

For me, following boarding life was tremendously difficult—like waking up at 5:30, going for fitness, having a bath full of stress, and going to school, being busy in school for 8 hours, having only a 10-minute rest, and then... going for sports was too stressful for me. It was just too much for me. The most difficult task—not only for me but for everyone—was following the routine strictly.

It was obvious that none of us wanted to follow the routine strictly, but one lady made us do that. I think I already gave a very deep introduction about her, and I think I don't need to remind you of her name again.

Chapter 5: Growing into the Routine

For new students, calling parents felt like World War III. Everyone fought for a few minutes on the phone. Old students made fun of us. Slowly, though, I began adjusting.

Most of the new students were desperate to talk to their parents, while the old students enjoyed watching us panic.

As I had climbed halfway up the mountain of boarding life, I slowly started to feel happy. I was adjusting to the new environment, far away from home. I've always been fond of watching movies— it's one of my favourite things to do in my free time. Every Sunday, during our free time, we had Television Time. Everyone used to fight for a spot on the sofa. I never felt like joining the fight, so I would quietly take a chair and sit next to the sofa. Later, everyone started copying my idea.

I was never very good at sports, but somehow, I managed to get through. Then came the toughest and hottest week—the last week of April. I heard that if the temperature crossed 42°C, we would get summer holidays. Every hour, I would check the weather on the computer, but the highest it went was 41.5°C. I was disappointed again...

Chapter 6: Summer and Snacks

As the summer holidays commenced, I was too excited to reach home. It took four hours from my boarding school to get there, and those four hours were the most anxious ones I had ever experienced. Last year, I was studying in the CBSE board, but after moving to this boarding school, I had switched to the ICSE board, which meant facing many new academic challenges.

I had also decided to finish my summer vacation homework and cover one-fourth of the syllabus for the Half-Yearly exams. I thought I was studying too much because I was carrying two bags full of books, while none of my friends had taken any books home. I was the only one carrying the entire load of books, and it almost felt foolish. But I loved studying, unlike most others who hated it. I would bring all my stuff home, whether it was a one-week or two-week holiday, while others only carried clothes. Some didn't even take their uniforms home, saying, "There's no use for them at home."

In boarding, we were all tired of living without snacks because they weren't allowed inside. But somehow—till today, I don't know how—some students managed to keep thirty packets of chips inside their cupboards. It remains one of the biggest mysteries of boarding life. The only possible way we thought was through the day boarders, who might be sneaking in tucks for them. We had no clue how they managed to sneak them in.

Since mobile phones are not allowed in boarding house, so whenever we went home, our favourite hobby became just using mobile phones. Dry fruits weren't allowed either. They were to be kept with Shubhra Ma'am, and she would give them to us every morning. But I often felt hungry in the evenings, so I secretly kept some dry fruits with me.

One day, some water got spilled in my cashews, and I knew they would spoil. I wanted to dry them in the sun, but I couldn't do it publicly. It was Sunday morning, and I was ready to complete my secret mission. I sat in the sun with a napkin in my hands and plenty of cashews spread out. Only two minutes had passed when I heard footsteps. I thought it was some seniors returning from sports, but when I looked up, it was Shubhra Ma'am!!!!!!

I was terrified. I thought if she found the cashews in my lap, she would throw them all away. But she seemed to be in a good mood that day. I quickly covered the cashews with my napkin and went back to my room, keeping them safely inside the cupboard. I was laughing internally the whole time, feeling like I had just completed a secret mission successfully.

Now, when I think back about those moments, I realise that they are some of the golden memories I am collecting. They seemed silly and stressful back then, but today, they are my fondest memories to be cherished for my whole life.

Chapter 7: Suitcases, Souvenirs, and Stories

Now it's been three years in boarding, and these years have given me not just discipline and independence, but also the chance to travel and explore the world beyond the campus. The first international trip I ever went on was with my parents—to Dubai. That trip gave me a lot of exposure. As an independent boy, I loved the experience. Dubai was full of tall buildings, shiny malls, and amazing places to visit. We saw the Burj Khalifa and even went on a desert safari. It was so different from India. That trip made me realise how much I enjoyed discovering new places.

But the most unforgettable trip for me was the one I took with my school friends—to Japan. That was the farthest I had ever travelled till now, and my first international trip with friends, which made it even more special. I was too excited even before we boarded the flight. I had so many things in my mind—Japanese food, snow, new friends, and of course, Mount Fuji.

In Japan, everything felt neat, clean, and well-organised. I found the Japanese culture very interesting and exciting. The people were extremely polite, and their way of speaking, dressing, and even bowing was new for me. We visited a school in Japan, and the students there were so friendly that it didn't even feel like we were in a foreign country. They greeted us warmly, played with us, and even tried speaking in English to make us feel comfortable. I made many new friends there. This is one picture with some Japanese friends that I keep with me.

One of the best parts of the trip was visiting Universal Studios. As a huge Harry Potter fan, it had been my dream to visit Hogwarts, and finally, it came true. I felt like I was living in the Harry Potter world. That was the moment I felt truly magical.

Another amazing place we visited was Mount Fuji. I was really hoping to see snow there, but unfortunately, there was no snow when we went. Still, it was freezing cold and beautiful. The view from there was stunning, and the air was so fresh. I felt like I was on top of the world.

Before Japan trip, I had already gone on three boarding school trips within India— Mumbai, Chandigarh, and Hyderabad. All of them were full of fun and learning, but the trip to Hyderabad was very special to me because I had a lovely photo with Shubhra Ma'am from that trip. She looked so different in that photo—smiling, relaxed, and proud.

Apart from travelling, these three years of boarding have also taught me how to be more organised than my siblings at home. I wake up at 5 AM without fail—a record I could never keep at home! I learnt many structured sports that I wouldn't have learned otherwise. Boarding life made me independent to do my own things—from arranging my books to managing time and taking care of my own needs.

In boarding house once a month, we were taken to DB Mall, a famous mall in Bhopal. I would always look for shops that sold small souvenirs so I could buy gifts for my family. From all these experiences, I learnt some of the most important lessons of life—like how to handle money, how to save, and how valuable even a small amount can be. Travelling with friends and family taught me how to explore the world with open eyes but boarding taught me how to explore myself.

Chapter 8: Steps from Silence to Stage

Before I joined boarding, I was learning abacus. It had only been a month, but I was enjoying it a lot. I still remember going to the UCMAS State Level Tournament in Indore. I gave my best but missed the merit award by just one rank. That failure hurt a lot. All my friends got prizes—big or small—they got something, but I came home empty-handed.

Then I joined boarding, and another tournament came up—a National Level Abacus Competition, but this time under a different franchise. I was short on time, struggling with a new routine, new people, and no parents around. I still decided that I had to win this one. There was no option.

It was my first month in boarding, and I was already tired, homesick, and underconfident. I missed my parents so much that sometimes cried quietly. And strangely, my favourite thing to do while crying was studying. I could focus better, like all my emotions were turning into concentration.

To participate in the national tournament, I had to take special permission from Kamal Sir, our Head of Boarding. That was my first outing from boarding. I practiced hard. I had to solve 200 questions in 8 minutes—a huge challenge. I finished 3–4 practice sheets easily, but during the actual competition, my hands were trembling. Still, I did my best.

The next day, the results were announced I was the First Runner-Up! I got a trophy that reached up to my waist. I was smiling the whole day. When I returned, everyone at boarding celebrated my win. That day I truly realised—boarding is not just a place; it's a family. Every individual achievement is celebrated by all.

A few months later, I had the chance to participate in my first MUN—Model United Nations, held at Scindia Boys School, Gwalior, one of the best boarding schools in India. Though I was curious to explore the campus, the main purpose was MUN.

I was representing New Zealand in the WHO committee. I had a laptop, a phone, and everything needed to prepare—everything except time. Our schedule at boarding was packed. Waking up at 5:30 AM, attending 8 hours of school, 30 minutes break, remedials, prep time... and by 10 PM, I was already exhausted. But still, I managed. I used every free second to research my country, its healthcare policies, its role in global health—I had to prepare 360 degrees.

I was very nervous on Day 1. It was a completely new experience—formal dress, formal speeches, and students from so many schools. But soon, I started to enjoy. I made many new friends, I spoke confidently, and I even got a **Verbal Mention** in the committee!

That single appreciation gave me a lot of confidence—not just for the next MUNs, but also for speaking up in class, participating in events, and believing in myself. I wasn't just the boy who cried and studied in silence anymore—I was slowly becoming someone who was being heard.

MUN taught me how to present ideas, listen, and lead. Abacus taught me how to stay focused under pressure. Both gave me strength in different ways.

And even though I still struggle with sleep, time, and long routines at boarding, I've learned that success comes when you don't give up—even when you're tired. Even when you miss home. Even when you feel like you're the only one who cares.

Chapter 9: Dreams and Dedication

In November, our school hosts something very grand—Founders. It's like our annual function, filled with cultural programs, exhibitions, and lots of excitement. I was a part of the Media and Publication Club, and honestly, I enjoyed every bit of it. I made many friends and became a journalist in *Sanskaar Infobros*. I was gaining popularity, but something else was shining even brighter in my mind—the Founders Award.

During Founders, Shweta Ma'am, my English teacher was the in-charge of our club. Although I had been in the school for eight months, I still didn't know her well at the beginning. But very soon, she became one of the biggest supports for me. She helped me not only with preparing for exams but also guided me in editing this very book. Her encouragement and belief in me made a big difference in my confidence.

It was my first Founders, so I didn't know much about the awards. But the one that caught my eye and captured my heart was Consistent Academic Excellence. The moment I saw Sarvagya Bhaiya, one of my senior receive that award, I was amazed. His respect among teachers and students grew like gold stocks rising! I knew, at that moment, that I wanted that award more than anything.

But there was a big problem. To get it, I needed a minimum aggregate of 90%, and I had only scored 83% in my Half-Yearly exams. To reach the target, I would need an almost impossible 93% in the Year-End exams. Still, I told myself, *"Let's give more than 100%."*

And I did. I studied with everything I had. As a first-year boarder, it wasn't easy—waking up early, juggling prep time, classes, and missing home. I felt both proud and stressed. When the results came out, I had scored 89.5%. I missed the mark, but I didn't lose hope.

In my second year, I came back stronger. I scored 91% in the Half-Yearly and 94% in the Year-End exams. This time, I was confident. But still, when the list for the award was announced the first time and my name wasn't there, I was heartbroken.

Then came the second list.

And there it was.

My name.

I was literally on cloud nine. I had done it. I had earned the award I had dreamt of for two whole years. That feeling can't be described—it was a mix of pride, relief, and something very emotional.

Behind this success were not just marks or hard work—but my parents. They were the true heroes. It's never easy for a parent to send their child away to a boarding school. I can't imagine the strength they had. Every struggle I faced, they felt it too. But their belief in me gave me strength. Their silent support was my loudest motivation.

And of course, Vaishali Ma'am, our house master who kept guiding me silently through it all— without expecting anything back.

That award didn't just prove I was a good student. It proved I had grown!

Chapter 10: The Shift, The Silence, and Something New

These three years of boarding have given me not just lessons but also people I can never forget. One of them is Yash—my closest friend, my biggest support. Another one is Krishna, who joined last year and quickly became a part of my small world. With them, boarding felt like home.

As I sit and write this book, flipping through my memories like pages of an old diary, I see a mountain of problems I've faced. And every time I ask myself: "How did I do that?" I really don't know. But I did.

And now, just when I thought I was getting used to everything, another change knocked on the door.

I've recently shifted to the Cambridge curriculum, leaving ICSE behind. This is the second shift in my academic journey. It was mostly my parents' decision—but also a little bit mine. They trusted me, and I want to prove them right. Once again.

But I won't lie—I'm scared!!!!

The class is new, the faces are new, and the friends are not the same.

Nobody from boarding is in the Cambridge class.
Not even Yash or Krishna.

They're still in ICSE, and I'm alone here.

I am introspective!! I am doubtful!!! I am
nervous!!!

But somewhere deep down, I am also hopeful.

Because if I could survive homesickness, 5:30 AM
alarms, lost notebooks, tough competitions, strict
wardens, and crushing routine...

Then maybe—just maybe—I can survive this too.

I've done many things that felt impossible. Maybe
this is just one more chapter of my boarding life...

The air feels different now.

The desk is unfamiliar.

So are the people.

But the pages are blank again—

And I've learned, sometimes,

a blank page is not empty.

It's full of possibility.

Nikhar is a young student and enthusiastic writer who finds joy in exploring the world through words. A boarding school student, he draws inspiration from everyday experiences and believes in turning memories into meaningful stories. Whether he's writing poems, sketching, reading books, or playing sports, Nikhar is always curious about the world around him.

Writing, for him, is not just a hobby—it's a way to dream big and give shape to his thoughts. When he's not studying or writing, you'll likely find him lost in music or enjoying a game with friends. This book is his heartfelt attempt to share the real, raw, and unforgettable journey of boarding life—with all its challenges, lessons, and golden moments.